I'm Not Broken Just A Little Twisted

Scenes

Through

The Mind of a Foster Child

_____

LaTasha C. Watts

I'm Not Broken Just A Little Twisted

Author's Note: This is a work of nonfiction. The events and experiences are all true and have been derived from my childhood journals, poems, drawings, as well as my memory. All pictures that you see, permission to use, was granted by all parties. However, names, identities and some circumstances have been altered, in order to protect the privacy of the various people involved in my story.

I'm Not Broken Just A Little Twisted
Copyright © 2012 by LaTasha C. Watts

Printed in the United Stated of America
Published by Cummings Watts & Associates, LLC
16781 Chagrin Boulevard, Number 129
Shaker Heights, Ohio 44120
ISBN 978-0-615-51919-7
Library of Congress Control Number: 2011914497

Dedication

For My "Jellybean" Ashley & "My Mel"
Thank you both for untwisting me
Without God sending me, you
I would have surely been broken.

I will love you both always!

**I'm Not Broken Just A Little Twisted
Scenes Through The Mind Of A Foster Child**

Hello Readers

In 2009, I came across a storage box full of journals, poems, letters and hand-drawn pictures. As I began to read each journal, I would soon discover that my childhood in foster care was right there in front of me. Gone were the days of not knowing why, in my adult life, I would feel so much pain, distrust and misery. The more I read through the journals, the deeper my "hidden" depression would rise. The more I read, the more I cried, the more I read, the further I would want to hide. This time in my life became so intense, that everything around me instantly stopped making sense. It was at this point that I felt the only thing that could save me was God and some good old fashion therapy.

As I began my talks with God and my long journey to weekly therapy sessions, I would soon discover that even though I felt like I had it all: a dream job, a home and my greatest achievement, my very own family, there was still some things missing inside me, and to my surprise those things were healing, forgiveness and inner peace. I realized that all these years, long after being in the foster care system, I had been covering up all of that pain and misery inside me. After those long talks with God and spending many days in therapy, I was able to forgive, truly find happiness and embrace my new found inner peace. I realize that every day is not going to be the greatest, but at least I don't have to spend those days in misery. So it is for this reason that I have chosen to open up my life to you, through a series of real-life experiences, in my journal entries. I realize that many of you may have gone through similar circumstances, and I wanted to let you know that you are not alone; and you can and will, one day, find inner peace.

Most people wake up each day with a mom, a dad or some form of a family structure. However, for some of us in the foster care system the reality of this type of life is few and far between. I barely remember important parts of my life, it's as if those parts never existed, and a whole section of my life just disappeared. I entered the foster care system as an infant, and my childhood would forever remain "chained" there. I was never adopted, and in my mind I grew up feeling that no one ever wanted me; as a result, I would spend my entire childhood drifting in out of relationships and struggling to grasp the concept of life, trust and most of all, family.

This Is My Story...

Chapter 1 - The Lost One

I was born on June 6, and I think it's 1973, at 12:42 a.m. I am not certain of the year because I am holding in my hand two very different birth certificates (which will become the subject of controversy throughout my adolescence). On one, I am born in 1972, the other 1973. On one, my mom is 17, and the other she is 16. This is a nightmare! It is bad enough that I am blind, burned and abused; at least I know those things. But to not know where I come from, and when I was actually born, is completely unheard of. I am so confused, my thoughts are just criss-crossing through my mind…Wow, just another stupid day, in the life of me.

The Lost One *(Poem)*

I am standing on the edge of complication.

Wondering why is it that my broken mind won't set me free?
I am standing on the edge of difficulty.

My mind not understanding why confusion
has became a hard part of me.

I am standing on the edge, Oh so close to victory.
My mind is a ramble closed with uncertainty,
watching that thing life walk right pass me.

Don't know who I am
But I am surely standing on the edge of misery.

A Foster Mother's Love *April 1983* (Age 9)

Today was a good day. I stepped outside of my apartment door, and the air was filled with the fresh smell of Downy, my favorite scent coming from the creepy laundry room. I call it the creepy laundry room because there isn't much light down there, just a bunch of cobwebs and tons of older kids smoking and drinking "yuck." Mommy and my sisters are gone shopping for me again. That means more purple clothes! I cannot wait until they get back, I am going to help her "snap" peas and cook in the kitchen today. I am so happy! I love my mommy! She is always doing nice things for me like: hugging me all the time, and telling how I am "such a special little girl." She even tucks me in at night! I love her so much!

The Year That Changed Everything
April 1984 (Age 10)

I am tired of being alone! I woke up this morning, and everyone is gone again! I am very hungry, and it is cold in my house! I wanted to wash up and put on some clean clothes, but I couldn't find any. All of my clothes are in the dirty clothes hamper. The good news is that there is food in the cabinet and in the refrigerator, so I guess I will be making my own food again. I must say I am starting not to like chicken noodle soup and hot dogs. I even walked downstairs to the creepy laundry room today. I wanted to see if someone would help me wash my clothes, but no one was there. I had to wash my underwear out in the bathroom sink, just like I did yesterday. Well I don't know what's going on around here, but I don't like it.

That Lady is Crazy – *April 1984* (Age10)

I was at school today, minding my own business, drawing at my desk when the principal came to get me out of class. I was so scared. So I walked as slow as I could, behind her. I thought whatever I did it had to be pretty bad, seeing that the principal had to come and get me. When we finally reached the doorway of her office there stood a tall white lady, with short dark hair, looking at me as if she had seen a ghost. She began to ask me a bunch of questions like: Did I know what a social worker was? Where did I live? Was my mommy at home? Was I hungry? She kept asking me so many questions, that I couldn't even answer one. The only thing I could do was cry. With all the tears streaming down my face, the entire room began to look like a blur. The principal handed me some tissues and told me that everything was going to be okay. She told me that the tall white lady with the short dark hair was my social worker and that they had been looking for me.

I just stared at the principal, wiped my face with my tissues and, as loud as I could I yelled, "That lady is crazy, I'm not lost, so stop looking for me!" I was so scared and confused, and I really did not know what to do. So I just sat there in the principal's office staring at the social worker and her staring back at me. I thought to myself, well maybe she wants to have a staring contest, so if I stare long enough maybe she'll blink.

Finally, the social worker opened her thin lips to speak. She said that she was sorry and that she didn't mean to upset me. The principal came over to my chair and asked me if I wanted McDonald's, now of course I said yes. I was so hungry and sick of searching to find whatever food I could eat. The social worker told me that she would get me a Happy Meal, but I needed to listen, answer all her questions and be good. I was so hungry that my mouth began to water, and the thought of getting a Happy Meal, almost made me want to cry again. So I just sat there and nodded my head and just like that, the principal opened the bottom drawer of her desk and handed me a Happy Meal. How and what magic she used to do that, I honestly didn't care, I just wanted to eat it.

While I was eating, the social worker told me about another family that wanted me. A family that would take me to Disney World, Cedar Point and even to the movies; it sounded like a lot of fun, but I told her no thank you because I knew that my mommy and sisters could take me. She told me that I could have two families and that I could live with one and have my own room, take trips to Disney World, Cedar Point and even to the movies. She even had the nerve to tell me that I could come back and visit my mommy and my sisters anytime that I wanted. She kept asking me over and over again "would I like that?" I never said a word, I just kept eating my Happy Meal. The social worker said that she was going to call my mommy, to see if it was okay for me to leave with her today; and just like that she got up and left the room. The whole time she was talking to me, I never answered her...I just gobbled up my food and kept singing over and over in my head, "this white lady is crazy."

I Told You That Lady Was Crazy
April 1984 (Age 10)

I knew it! I knew it! I told you that white lady was crazy! When she came back into the room, she told me that I could go home and that she would seeing me again real soon. I could not wait to get out of that principal's office! As soon as that bell rang, I ran straight for the coat room, only having the hall

14

monitor to yell "stop running," one time. I grabbed my coat and ran straight for the door. I swear it seemed like it took me forever to walk up the hill to my house. When I finally reached the top of the hill, I could see my mommy looking out the window as if she was waiting on me. I rushed through the door, ran up the steps, and told her all about the social worker and her crazy story. My mommy gave me a hug and said "don't worry." I would have bet my favorite pair of purple pants, just to prove that I knew that lady was crazy!

The Day Time Stood Still – *April 1984* (Age 10)

Today started off with my mommy waking me up with lots of hugs and kisses! Running into my room after that was my sister, with her tickle fight. I just knew that today was going to be a good day! I could smell the aroma of bacon and pancakes filling the air...Yummy! I got out of my bed and went into the kitchen. For breakfast, I had all of my favorites grits, cheese eggs, bacon and pancakes. It was a good day because everyone was at home, both of my sisters, my nephew and even my cousins stopped by. We played and ate all of my favorite foods all day. Mommy even let me bake my favorite recipe, chocolate syrup and peanut butter cupcakes. Mommy kept saying that today was a special day. When I asked her "what made today so special," she looked at me and began to cry. She told me that today would be my last day with her, and that the social worker was coming to get me. I now have to live with a new family.

I just crumbled to the floor like a balled-up piece paper and began kicking, screaming and yelling as loud as I could, "Why?" "Why?" I cried, "Don't you love me?" Mommy pulled me up off the floor and began to hug me real tight and told me that she will always love me and that everything was going to be all right. My sisters came running into the bedroom, where we all began to cry. I love my family, and I do not understand why I have to leave! That mean social worker lied to me! I hate her! Why is she taking me away from my family!

Mommy said that there was nothing that she could do and that this is what was best for me. She told me to stop crying and to hold my head up high and that no matter what...we would see each other real soon. When things began to settle down, which seemed like it took forever, the packing began. In slow motion, one by one, the dresser drawers opened and into the garbage bags my life went. I felt just like garbage that was being thrown away; "off to a new family I (the garbage) would be sent."

The Poetic Garbage Was Collected At The Door
April 1984 (Age 10)

When the social worker came to get me, she was not alone. There was a fat, dumpy white man, with a gross-looking beard, who just stood at the door, looking evil and weird. He grabbed my garbage bags as if he was taking them to the trash, I watched him drag everything I owned down the hall until he disappeared. I then ran to my mommy and sisters and hugged them, with tears streaming down my face, I had no choice but to say good-bye. I wanted to scream, kick and yell! I opened my mouth, but my voice was empty. I wished that God would have saved me with every tear that I cried. I know it in my heart that this is the final goodbye, and I will never see them again!

The Garbage Has Arrived, With No Explanation
April 1984 (Age 10)

As I sat in the back seat of the car, on my way going to my new family's house, all I could do was pretend to fall asleep. I figured at least this way the social worker would "shut up" and stop talking to me. As I laid there pretending to be asleep, I began to remember all of my good times, and it made me feel a little happy. As the car continued to move down the street, I could hear the social worker and the dumpy man whispering about me.

The social worker said that the agency had lost track of me and that if it weren't for someone at the school filing a complaint, they would have had no idea when they would have found me. What is she talking about? Agency? Complaint? And there's that damn word LOST again! She said that my mommy had stopped cashing some checks and that she did not report to the agency that we had moved. I learned that I had missed quite a bit of school and would be repeating a grade in my new place.

As we turned down a street, the social worker leaned over from her seat and whispered to me, "we are almost here." So I pretended to wake up very slowly. As I sat up, I could feel my heartbeat nearly pounding out of my chest. I could hear every sound around me and at this point every sound sounded sooooo loud and scary; from the cars going past, to a dog I keep hearing barking on the street. I finally opened my eyes and begin to peak out of the car window. I now know without a doubt I am really scared. The people on this street look different and scary. We pulled up to the driveway of my new house and there stood this light-skinned lady, waving and smiling at us. As the car stopped, I opened the door and at the moment I felt like, "it's time to take the garbage out." I didn't say a word; I slid to the edge of my seat, heart pounding, with my tears sucked back into my mind because I was so scared. I took one foot and put it slowly to the ground and then the other. I stood up and stared at the ground, with my fist balled up so tight, that I could feel my finger nails pressing against my palms. This is a feeling that I have never had before and one that I can not explain! BUT I now know this…things will never be the same.

Still No Explanation *April 1984* ^(Age10)

I stood there outside of the car as if I was on display, with the neighbors and this lady looking at me. She said hello and introduced herself as if I cared, I just really wanted my mommy, and I was still scared. The dumpy man lugged my things up the stairs and onto the front of the porch. She told the man to leave my bags there and invited us in. I just stood there and couldn't move, I felt like a limp pickle the kind that no one wants, so I just stood there staring at my garbage bags, right there on the front of the porch.

When I did decide to enter the house, I slowly opened the door and saw the light-skinned lady, the social worker and the dumpy man all sitting on a couch. And for the first time since all this nonsense began, the social worker asked me if I had any questions and if I understood why I was there. I just looked at her and asked "is this the family that's taking me to Disney World, and then I could go back home?" She never answered my question; she just kept rubbing my shoulders and telling me that everything was going to be okay and that it would take some time for me to adjust to the change. And with that, the tall white lady with the short dark hair and the fat, dumpy man stood up, said their goodbyes and left me right there, scared, confused and with no explanation!

Your Garbage Is Garbage *April 1984* ^(Age10)

When the social worker left I just stood on the porch, standing next to my garbage bags, staring at her car until it drove out of sight. The light-skinned lady said her name was Ms.

Lawson and that she would show me to my room. As I went to grab my garbage bags of everything that I owned, Ms. Lawson looked at me and said "oh no honey, you can put those _thangs_ into the garage, they are not coming into my house." _Thangs?_ I think is a word for something you can not stand or just plain hate. So there I was with my entire life inside a few garbage bags _(my thangs)_, dragging them down her long driveway to be put into her garage, just like the garbage that I am, and they are!

Chapter 2 – **This Is My Existence**

My Existence (poem)
Would you notice me if I was not there?
Would you make that observation or would you even care?
Or Am I that distant memory,
That only makes a noise upon your mental request.
Or Am I that functional character,
That you recognize only to show your best.

At Least I Have My Purple Pants *May 1984*

(Age10)   A month has passed by since I last wrote. I still miss my real family, more than anyone will ever know (I still call them my real family even though I now know they were a foster family too). Ms. Lawson is loud and cusses when she gets mad which is not hard to see her do. So I usually just cover my ears and go in my room.

As for my things, after a few days I was allowed into the garage to them, but when I got there everything was a mess. My garbage bags were torn open and my clothes were hanging out everywhere! Everything I owned was thrown around the garage on display. On top of that Ms. Lawson told me that I am getting all new things and that I had to pick and choose what I wanted and then she decided what could stay! Who in the hell does she think she is? Messing with my things! I had to go through all of my stuff and throw away just about everything. I wish I could have seen the look on my face. There I was, sitting in the garage, on my knees, picking through my own stuff, as if I was at a garage sale. Oh! How the tears wanted to come, but I refuse to let them in. I just grabbed a few things, including my favorite pair of purple pants; I pulled those pants out of the garbage bag, held on tight and quickly put them over my shorts. I said to myself, "She will not get these, these belong to me!"

Closure So I Can Be Free *October 1986*

(Age13) It has been hard for me to be here so long. I now have a new social worker and I finally started to call Ms. Lawson "Ma." It was kind of weird at first, because I felt that I was not being loyal to my old family, but I wanted to fit in and be a part of some family.

Things have been crazy, I must admit. Since I have been here, I learned what social workers were, about agencies and psychologist, and what being a foster child really meant; but none of that mattered because to me, it means only one thing, that I belong to nobody. Things have just been downhill, especially ever since I had access to use the telephone. I have been sneaking and talking to my sisters from my old family, every chance I get. I mean, what do people expect for me to do? Just adjust and forget.

I learned a lot from these phone calls, I finally found out why I had to leave. My sisters told me that I lived with them as a foster child for almost nine years, and was loved and taken care of very well. Until one day, when we moved and just disappeared from the agency's radar without a trace. My mother had stopped cashing the agency checks, and I missed an entire year of school. My sisters were much older and had moved out of the house and became aware of the situation when it was way too late. All of this happened because my mother was sick with a disease called Alzheimer's which made her forget important things (like taking care of me).

I also learned that my sisters would be moving away and that my mother would be placed in a nursing home, where she could be safe. They told me that they loved me and for me to keep being strong. They vowed to find me in the future, when I was a lot older and could better understand the situation. And just like that, the only family I knew was gone again.

I know that my sisters love me, and I am sad that my mother is sick, I know deep in my heart, she will always love me and that I know for sure she will never forget!

I Just Don't Fit
November 1986 (Age13)

I've been here for awhile now and things are still the same. There are some good times and bad days. My new sister treats me good, but can sometimes be a grouch. She has a son, he likes me some times, but he always gets away with being mean to me. He is just a "spoiled little brat." He has a little brother and I love him so much, I also get to babysit him often. Then there comes my grandmother, she is the controller of the house, what she says is the law.

I also have a cousin, who lives in another state. She visits every summer and during her visit she gets treated like a queen. All I can do is just sit back and watch her get everything. Although, when she does come to town we do have a lot of fun, but at the end of the day, the family shows me that she will always be number one! Ma is okay, she is cool when she is not cussing and yelling at everything little I do. She has a boyfriend now and he seems like he is all right. However, through the good and the bad, no one will ever understand how I feel. I feel like an outsider, not really belonging to a family. I am sad, just about all the time. I can't explain it, and I know it's crazy, but I just don't belong here, I just don't fit anywhere.

Why Would Someone Want To love Me
December 1986 (Age13)

I am still here, same crap different day! Some days are good and some days are bad. I wish I could just run far, far away from here, and keep running until somebody loves me! My real family (biological) didn't love me; if they did I wouldn't even be in foster care! The way I hear it and from what I see my real mother tried to kill me! She left me burned and scarred for life, hell I can't even see. Maybe they left me because I am ugly. Hell I would leave me too, JUST LOOK at me! I wear these stupid pop bottle glasses and have acne all over my face, the girls and the boys all make fun of me!

I remember, about a year ago, I used to be friends with this boy named Kenny, who lived down the street. He used to come over, and we would hang out on my porch. We would draw, play games and sometimes even dance and sing until nightfall. But that all changed when people on the street started to tease him about hanging with me. This included my next door neighbor, who even had a pet name for me: "blind eye-jet-eye is so ugly." After that we weren't friends anymore. He even had the nerve to tell me, "you're cool, but I can't hang around you because of what people might think."

There was also a new girl on the street, Rochelle, who everyone loved, except me! Last night we were all at her house, it was me, my cousin and some other people on the street. We were sitting back drinking some kool-aid and ice tea. So she thought that it would be okay to fill my cup up with pee. Just when I was about to drink it, I mean cup to my lips, my cousin grabbed it laughing and poured it out. Why do people think that it is okay to hurt me? Haven't I been through enough?

24

I feel like I'm surrounded by a whole bunch of enemies, without one single person interested in giving me an ounce of love. Don't I deserve to be loved? Where in the hell is my family?

Change Is Good
February 1988 (Age14)

Well it's February, Ma and I have finally moved, to the suburbs and I love it here! The people are nice, and it is what I call a "mixed breed," black, white and anything in-between. I feel like a new me. Absolutely no one knows me here! I can start all over with a new identity. Ma got married to her boyfriend, and he is extra nice. He spoils me to death, and I love it! Believe it or not I actually call him dad. He always brings me things home when he comes in from work, like candy, pickles and even my favorite hot popcorn. He even bought me a brand new bike! It's now just him, my mom and me. Wow! I think we just might be a family.

Now all I need to do is find me some new friends around the neighborhood (who know nothing about the old me) and then my life will be complete. Ahhhh...CHANGE IS Soooo Good!!

Yes! I Finally Found You
July 1988 (Age15)

I have been looking for you all over the place! I thought some nosy person found you, read you and then threw you away! Man a lot has happened since I last wrote in here. Things at home are "all good," Mom and I are getting along, I have not been on punishment in a long time. Yelling has somewhat became a thing of the past (thank goodness for that). I met a lot of new friends; I even have a few boys looking at me. Cute ones at that! My new school is cool too. I am VP of student council, and I even run track (even though no ever comes to see me run). I even started showing off my MC skills (you know NO one can beat me). I have all the fresh rhymes and poetry. Life is good, and I am a brand new me!

Wow! Tell Me What You Really Think
August 1988 (Age15)

Well it's been about a month since I last wrote in here. It's not that I am abandoning my journal. I just have to keep coming up with clever ways to keep you hidden. There are a few new additions to the household, and they are nosy and thieves. It's all my fault, all I did was ask for a LITTLE sister, someone younger than me; next thing you know it has turned into foster care central up in this place. There have been a few little boys and even some girls.

Then came Charlie and she changed everything! Charlie I think is 16; she is mixed with Italian and black, with long hair. She had a baby already before she got here. Charlie at first seemed real nice, but she was sneaky as hell! She smoked cigarettes, drank and even smoked weed. Ever since her arrival I have become second best. I know this for sure because I overheard my foster dad and mom talking about me.

We were in the car, and I was pretending to be asleep (like I always do). My foster dad was driving, and my mom was sitting in the passenger's seat, she whispered to him "Charlie is so cute isn't she?" My foster dad said, "Yes she is a pretty girl." She then leaned over and whispered to him, "that one in the back is becoming cute, but we had to put a lot of work in her." Now I am just lying there, quiet and trying not to move, all the while I am thinking to myself...What was that supposed to mean? She then continued on with this story. The more I listened the madder I got; she talked about when I first came and how raggedy I was. I even learned about her prior visits with the agency and how they showed her this pretty girl that she thought she was going to get. But then I showed up, and she was disappointed because I was raggedy with short hair. She even went on to say that she thought to herself "what am I suppose to do with that!" That! That! I wanted to say something so bad, but I couldn't. What the hell is she talking about THAT?!! I know I am not a beauty queen. Charlie uses her looks to get and do everything! Everyone thinks that she is the shit! That is one car ride that I wish I wasn't pretending and that I really was asleep. Here I thought, I was finally relaxing, and things were going well. What a joke! Now I really know what they think...

This is what I actually looked like
when I first came to Ms. Lawson's home.
This picture was taken at school a few weeks before.

Chapter 3 – Can You Hear Me

Listen (Poem)

Listen can you hear me?
Or is it that my problems of life are only at their greatest
if they are portrayed as a self help novelty.

Seriously you can't hear me?
My cries for help can only remain in my mind secluded
and drowning in self pain and misery
that are not allowed to exist in reality.

You refuse to hear me trumping my pain
for your own, so you can sit comfortably.
Hear me without ill intent
Listen to my cries without resentment.

Are you serious, you really can't hear me?
I am screaming so loud being filled with doubt
and my mind with misery.
And you really can't hear me?

Well If You Can't Beat'em Then Join'em
October 1988 ^(Age15)

I have decided to become cool with Charlie although I still don't trust her. She has got everyone in the neighborhood fooled. So instead of causing trouble, I have just decided to blend in. Besides, hanging with Charlie makes everything in my life run smoother.

I get to stay out late and chill with the boys, while Charlie just sits back drinking beer and smoking weed. Me, I just sit back and drink a beer every now and then. I know what you're thinking, what the hell, right? But it's cool, Charlie tells me every day, "you can't be a pussy if you're gonna hang with me." So I just shut up and go. Sometimes we even chill behind the bleachers at school, I even tried some weed a few times, but I didn't like it. Weed is definitely not my style. So I guess I will just stick to drinking beer or whatever the alcohol of the week is.

Whenever I drink, it makes me feel so free! I just drink and drink and then fly away to any place that I want to be. Sometimes I pretend to fly away to find my parents, hell maybe they're looking for me. It's crazy how we can get liquor anytime we want. You'll never guess who buys it, and all we have to do is ask.

I even have a boyfriend now, which Charlie knows all about. Quiet as kept, I have had at least two boyfriends since I moved here. Anyway, this one is fine as hell, his name is Mason. He lives a few blocks over from me. We have been going together off and on for some time. He likes me, but hates that the other boys in the neighborhood love to hang around me. Between you and me Mason has been in my house and even in my bedroom. We kiss a lot and even hold hands, no sex yet, but that's in the plan. First I have to make sure that he loves me. My goal is to find someone who will love me and "I will find that person real soon."

Trying To Control The Storm
December 1988 (age15)

Well the hell with this bullshit! My foster mother than flipped her lid! Once again she is trying to control me and put me back in my quiet little shell. But not this time, I am too far out to let her stuff me back in! Back into a world where I have no friends and I am considered the ugliest thing on the street! I refuse to go back. I have come too far! I have lots of friends, I hang out with Charlie, and Charlie's got my back. I get good grades, I do my chores, and the police are never at the door for me! What else does she want from me? Just look at her running around here, yelling and cussing. She must be crazy! Saying "No more boy phone calls" and telling me that I have to hang around nothing but girls. This is some bullshit! Just because a lot of boys hang around me, don't make me a whore. I know it looks bad, I agree, but forget that, I'm going to be me. She is not my real mother, she can't control me!

My real mother can "kick rocks," she abused me and left me damaged for life! I am stuck in foster care, messed up, confused and hurting, every time I think about what she did to me! I have to grow up with fake ass parents…Hell I don't even know what my real parents look like, or even if I have brothers or sisters. I know that I am not alone and that there are others out there, just like me, but alone is how I feel, and that feeling comes with a sharp pain that constantly stabs me.

I know people who don't know the reality of my situation here would probably say, "How could you say that, after all this lovely lady has done for you." Well that is a bunch of BULL-

31

SHIT! If anybody ever asked me to give some examples of the nonsense that I go through daily, I can name a few a mile long. The man of the house is not that cool, and she just called me a liar, a heifer and a sneaky little bitch, all while I am writing in you! Oh! If I could only tell you!

Something Is Not Right
December 31, 1988 *(age15)*

Well today is the last time we will see 1988, it has been a crazy year. The adults are all going out and the kids are staying home. So I know that we are going to have plenty of fun. My foster dad supplied us with everything that we need: money, alcohol and beer. The only thing missing is Charlie's weed. That's right! I wasn't going to say anything because mom doesn't know. My foster father has been giving us money and alcohol, ever since Charlie got here. The only thing we have to do is not tell anyone, give really big hugs, and kisses on the cheek. Around the neighborhood, we are known as the party house where the food and liquor is free!

We also have some new additions to the house. Now it's just me, the two new girls (Tami and Tyan), and Charlie. We are all around the same age, but unfortunately they still refer to me as the "baby." These girls are way more advanced than me. Everyone in the house has had sex, stolen things, and some of them have even spent time in Juvi. As for the famous Charlie, she is the leader of the pack. She has done it all and seen just about everything. At this point, I just categorize her as an all out freak! However, together the four of us are unstoppable, not to mention today we had so much fun! All of our friends on the street came over to chill, we drank, played loud music and people had weed. I even let Mason come over and you know he kept asking me for sex. My new sisters and Charlie were egging me on, but I was not about to give it up to that bum. Why? Because I know for a fact that he does not fully love me, quiet as kept, I caught him cheating on me. Yea that's right! But I keep him around anyway, some love is better than none. Anyway back to today, I was drunk as hell and it was a lot of fun. We had people everywhere, until my foster parents pulled up. It was hilarious, watching everyone scatter like roaches in a dark room, as if the lights were suddenly turned on. It was crazy! My foster parents were coming in the front door, while we were pushing people out the back door.

When they finally came in, you know we had to play it off. We ran up to them, laughing and screaming Happy New Year! We were hugging everyone, until my foster father began kissing us on the lips! It was weird, he said that it was an accident and that we moved our heads too quickly. Now that right there messed up everybody's high; especially mine, because for the rest of the night, all I could think about was how disgusting and uncomfortable it was. Later on, we all got together and talked about it, trying to figure out, how could it be possible that all of us moved our heads too quickly. Needless to say, we all went to bed tonight, feeling a little uneasy, but chalked the incident up as a mystery.

What Goes Up Must Come Down
January 1989 (Age15)

Well let's see, it's been about a month since I have written in here. Things have been completely CRAZY! For starters, Charlie is GONE! Basically she ran away and got pregnant, and the agency put her in some program, for pregnant teens. Tami went back to live with a relative (lucky). Which brings me to Tyan, she tried to commit suicide by taking a whole lot of sleeping pills. After taking the pills, she poured liquid dish soap on every floor in the house, except in front of my room. It all started late one night. I was sitting in my room and my mother screamed my name, I opened the door, and she said, "I think something is wrong with Tyan." As I began to look for her, I found her, walking around the house mumbling, and pouring dish soap everywhere. I just knew something was wrong.

I ran and called 911, I have never been so scared in my life! Ma tried to keep her calm. She kept trying to talk to Tyan as she walked around, but it really didn't help. She would just stop and stare at mom, with this blank scary look on her face. It was a mess. As we waited for the ambulance to arrive, Tyan kept trying to say something to me, but I could not understand her, it sounded like a bunch of mumbling. I kept telling her to "chill out" and that everything was going to be okay.

When the ambulance finally arrived, she was taken away very quickly. I had to stay home and cleaned up all that damn dish soap, while mom raced to the hospital. Later, I learned that Tyan would be just fine. She had to get her stomach pumped, but had only taken a few pills. The doctors say that she suffered a "Psychotic Break," due to stress and anxiety.

Psychotic Break, Tyan & Me
January 1989 (Age15)

Today I learned that Tyan will not be coming back. The agency will be placing her in a group home, and from what I heard it is one of the worst in the city.

I spoke to her yesterday, and she is scared as hell! I asked her flat out "why did you try to kill yourself, I mean is it really that bad?" She said that she felt alone and that she was tired of being mistreated and being dragged around like a dog. At that moment, I just sat on the phone and begin to cry.

I mean, I knew exactly how she felt. Being in foster care is a sad and lonely place to be. BUT I would never try to take my life over it. Then all of sudden, those tears of mine dried right up. I got mad, and I told her this: Sure the only family in our lives is basically being paid to be our FAKE family. Not to mention all of the crazy stories of abuse that we all share, BUT you are forgetting one thing…WE ARE STILL HERE! Our real families may not have wanted us, BUT we are still here! We can tell them all this, "You may not have wanted us BUT we don't need you!" "We can make something of ourselves WITHOUT YOU!" "It may take us longer, BUT WE ARE STILL HERE!" "Psychotic Break my Ass!" And that is actually what I told her!

After that, we just sat there on the phone quite, for a minute or two. When the silence ended, we began to talk and laugh about all of the stupid stuff we did while she was here. Eventually she had to get off the phone, but not before telling me that she was in counseling two times a week, plus a group session (In my head, I was like, Damn that's a lot). But I told her, "That was good" and to listen to the doctors, because they were there to help her. I am so glad that Tyan is getting the help that she needs. Because anything is better than dying! I am really going to miss her.

Looking For Peace
February 1989 (Age15)

Well it's just me for now, and I don't know how long it is going to last. Sooner or later it will be "foster care central" up in here again. And no telling how old they will be or what they will be like. Hopefully they will be a "calm foster crew," and not the "wild foster crew." So, for now I am enjoying my time of peace.

But I will say this, sometimes I do find myself a little sad because it's just me, but I dare not say anything; because I know that asking for a LITTLE sister definitely changed how my life used to be. So for now, if I get a little on edge, my foster father will get me some beer or something and that will surely keep me at peace.

Downward Spiral
March 1989 (Age15)

I have the worst hangover in the world this morning. My head hurts and I swear that every time I move, I am going to "earl." Not to mention, that mom is still yelling at me from yesterday. I swear that I am NEVER drinking again! Yesterday was scary enough as it is. I barely remember anything. I mean everything is really fuzzy.

This is how I remember my day: I was in the back yard, I had a few friends over, my foster dad bought us some wine, we drank the wine, he left in his car, my friends went home…and at least two hours later, I was laying flat on my stomach, in the backyard, in the grass, completely soaked in pee. Mom was standing at the backdoor screaming at me. "Where in the hell have you been?" "I have been calling you for hours!" When I looked at her and said, "In the backyard," her response was, "I looked back here and you were not in no damn backyard!"

Now here comes the scary part: I have no idea where I was, what I was doing, or who I was with! It's as if my entire afternoon had been erased! I have been trying to remember it, but I just can't. For the first time, I must say I am on a well-deserved punishment. I mean I could have been killed, kidnapped or even raped! What was I thinking? To top it off, when I did get in the house, I finished the rest of the wine, even spilling it on my table and cupping my hands to catch the dripping wine as it rolled off the edge of the table and on to a sheet. Next thing you know, it is the next day, and I am in my bed in the same clothes, still soaked with pee. WHAT IS WRONG WITH ME? Am I a drunk? Can I stop drinking? I think I might need a little help. I don't want to be a drunk at 15…that's it NO more drinking for me!

Innocence Almost Lost
April 1989 (Age15)

I don't know who to tell or what to do. I can't believe this shit actually happened to me. I trusted him, but I should have known better! Things around here have been a little fishy. I'm so scared right now, and I just know, that no one is going to believe me. Today I was just chill'in at home, doing some homework and watching some TV. I heard my mom's car rolling over the rocks in our gravel driveway as she left for choir rehearsal, like she does every week. Sometimes I tag along and just sit in the church pew reading or drawing. So today I decided to stay at home. It was just me, my foster father and our dog. No sooner than my mom left my foster father called me, I was like damn it! I'm trying to do my homework what does he want!

I walked down the stairs and stood at their bedroom door, and there he was lying on the bed in his boxer shorts with no shirt on. I thought to myself, "please but some damn clothes on." I asked him what did he want, and he said "can you come here?" I said "what do you need?" Now this right here is some shit, you would not believe…He said, "Come and lay with me." I think my face at that moment turned green. I felt so sick to my stomach, that I couldn't move, I couldn't even breathe. I just stood there for a moment frozen in time.

At first I thought maybe I misunderstood. NO, he made it real clear, when he got out of his bed and grabbed me from the back. He put both his hand on my breast and whispered, "Don't you remember when we brought in the New Year together, your lips were so soft and sweet." I just wanted to throw up, Oh! My God he really did try to kiss me! I managed to break loose, and I screamed, "GET OFF ME!"

I tried to run through the kitchen and to the back door, but he was so quick and really trying hard to catch me. I grabbed up the dog and put him in front of me as I backed out of the kitchen and moved toward the front door. I managed to make it past the dining room table, the whole time with him talking and touching all over me. He kept saying things like: "You owe me," "You bet not tell ya' momma, you're a liar, so who she gonna believe." He told me my worse fear, "If you do tell they will take you from here, you're a teenager you'll go straight to a group home." I was scared, with my heart pounding and knees stiff, I threw that dog at him and made a dash to the front door. I slammed it behind me and ran off my porch.

I ran down the driveway and broke into tears headed to my friend's house, pounding on her door. I was so scared! I looked across the street, at my house, and he was on the front porch yelling, "get in the house!"

Words can not express the fear in my heart as my friend opened her door, I just pushed right past her and started yelling, "SHUT THE DOOR!" As I ran in crying, I sat on her couch and told her everything. Her parents were not at home and we certainly did not know what to do. I wanted to call the police, but I was so scared and confused. We just called up the boys next door, hoping that they could help. Instead, they went to my house with bats and sticks, telling my foster father to "step outside," they were mad and ready to fight. He dared not step outside; the coward just stood in the doorway and did not say a word. I stayed next door until my mother got home.

When she arrived I damn near knocked her over as she got out of the car, but still too scared to say a word. I walked in the house shaking, with my heart still left at my friend's house across the street. When she came into the house, I was directly behind her, and he was just standing there, staring at me. My mom headed straight for the basement, I swear I was right on her heels, when all of a sudden he put his hand across the doorway and stopped me. My mother did not notice, so she kept on walking ahead of me. At this time I honestly didn't know what to think, or even what to do. He leaned in real close and whispered, "I won't do it again, please just don't tell on me, whatever you need you know I will get it for you, okay." I just stood there numb, realizing that the only father figure that I had ever known just betrayed me.

Keeping Me Safe
April 1989 (Age15)

It's been kind of quiet around here since the incident, with my mom's husband. I no longer call him "dad" or "foster dad," he does not deserve that respect! I don't speak to him, and he doesn't speak to me, and that's just the way I like it.

I replay that night over and over again in my head. I keep asking myself, "Why did he try to get me?"and "Am I the only one?" What's sad about all of this is that I believed that he was a "cool dad," but I realize now that all he ever wanted was to have sex with me. When he was chasing me around the house, he made me feel as if I owed him for all the things he had done for me. All of the money, gifts, hugs and free alcohol, I feel so dirty. Oh! I am so mad at myself, how come I couldn't see it? I have not told my mom, because I am too scared. At this point, I turn

16 in a few months and in two more years I will be 18. I will be GROWN and then I am OUT of here! So for now, I don't drink, smoke <u>NOTHING!!</u>

I never stay at home alone, and I purposely keep extremely busy. I joined a few clubs at school and even started a club of my own. I also became a community teen liaison, which is actually just a fancy name for teen volunteer. And when summer starts, I got that covered to: I will be starting a new job working at a restaurant and I have already requested the maximum summer hours to work there too. So if, by chance I have to be at home, you best believe if my mother gets up to go anywhere, I will damn near be a part of her shoe! I know she will hate it because sometimes she likes her space, but I don't care, because at least I'm safe!

Interruption from the author: The realization of my story is that <u>I did eventually tell</u>, and I am sad to report, that I was not the only one that he had done this to. I just happen to be one of the few who got away. It is <u>never</u> okay for <u>anyone</u> to touch you or to behave in an inappropriate manner. If you or someone that you know is in a situation like this, <u>tell someone you trust</u>, because <u>it's not your fault</u> and it is <u>never</u> okay!

Chapter 4 – It's A Family Affair

No Comfort in Me (poem written age 16)

The lost steps to find comfort pierce's my soul
The evil around us prevents us from being whole.

A Fashion Show Changed Everything

May 1989 (Age15)

Oh! My goodness, you would not believe what happened to me! Today I was in a fashion show for my mom's church thing. A lot of people were there from our church, but for some reason, I was still nervous. You would think since I see these people every Sunday, it would be a piece of cake, but not for me. Not to mention every time I walked down the runway, I noticed this lady smiling and staring at me. When the fashion show was over, at the reception the lady approached me. She asked me where were my parents and I pointed to my mother's seat. At first I thought I did something wrong, but realized I had never seen her before and that she didn't even know me.

They talked for quite a while and every now and they would point at me. Eventually my mom introduced her to me and without any warning, the lady said: "Hi my name is Maureen and I think I know your dad's side of your family." My heart sank to my chest with a feeling that you would not believe. Could it be? Does she really know my family?

The whole car ride home my mother started to prepare me: she said that she had the number of an aunt, that she would call first to see if she knew me. She also said that if she did, the outcome could go one of two ways; either they would want to get to know me or may not want to have anything to do with me. After that, she said nothing more.

41

I am lying here now, wondering all sorts of things: What do they look like? Who do I look like? What really happened to me? Or maybe I have a few siblings? The list just goes on and on.

Finding My Family
May 1989 (Age15)

Guess what, I found my family! Turns out that the lady Maureen was exactly right! She did know my dad's side of my family! It was crazy! It was as if I had stepped into the twilight zone and the shows were about me. The first person I talked to was my great aunt; turns out they have always been looking for me! They talked about me to anyone who would listen, so Ms. Maureen must have listened and listened carefully. She recognized me from the burns on my legs, my pop bottle glasses, and I still had my father's last name. The bottom line is that if my great aunt and the rest of my family did not talk about me as much as they did, I would have still been a distant memory.

This has been the greatest day of my life. I met my real biological father today and it was so crazy! He pulled up in our driveway, with a banana yellow colored Cadillac, and I am sure that I saw it speed around the corner on two wheels. As I stood in the walkway in front of our house, he hopped out of the car, I thought to myself, is it even in park? He ran up the walkway and hugged me with a face full of tears. I collapsed in his arms and just began to sob, and I asked to myself is this really real? For the first time in my life, today I am free, today I belong to someone, other than me.

Family Meeting

May 1989 (Age15)

Well today was a totally awesome day! I met what you would call my "immediate family." First of all my dad is a tall giant and very skinny. My great aunt is extremely short, and everyone says I look like her. Oh! My goodness! Are you ready for this, I have: a father, a mother (not the one who abused me), a brother, and finally a LITTLE sister (who favors me), a grandpa, a grandma, uncle and cousins, as far as I could see. Guess what? I finally belong to somebody, and that somebody is a family!

Putting The Rumors to REST

May 1989 (Age15)

Okay first off, finding my dad's side of the family put a lot of rumors to rest. So far I learned that my parents were married. Then they divorced, after all of the drama surrounding my abuse. After the divorce, my dad's side of the family cut almost all contact with my mom's side of the family. My dad also kept a copy of the original court documents, so that he could one day give them to me. So I learned the following: I was born in 1973 not 1972, It was proven that my mom did abuse me, and there was a nasty court battle, where both sides of the family tried to get custody of me. At the end of the day, no one won but the agency. And as we know the rest was history!

Getting To Know YOU

May 1989 (Age15)

My mom has allowed me to hang out with my real family, especially on the weekends. It has been real cool, we do things like go shopping and visit everyone under the sun. Everyone in the family seem so close and they're all touchy feely, every time they see me. But I don't mind, it just shows that they really did miss me. I even have a job now, working at a day care center every day afterschool and guess who takes me? My <u>REAL</u> father! I really enjoy hanging with my family, they are a lot of fun! And I believe in my heart that how they treat me is real and not phony.

At first I was worried about my foster mom because I did not want her to feel bad or jealous. Even though things are crazy around my house, she has been my mother. She has taken care of me for all these years, so I don't want to hurt her. As a matter of fact, in two months we are all going on a family vacation, with both families. Both families are so different (like night and day), so I know that this vacation to Canada is going to be CRAZY.

The Vacation Is Over

August 1989 (Age16)

Well our vacation to Canada started out awesome! We all left together but were in different cars. We even stopped to eat together. It was so much fun! I rode with my foster mom first and then with my real family. My grandpa has a van with a lot of room and even a TV. Heck, they even had this gigantic cooler, full of snacks, and to my surprise, they brought some for me. It was great! When we arrived at the hotel, we even had rooms on the same floor. So you know me, I ran back and forth between everybody's rooms. After settling in my real family wanted to go out, but my foster family was too tired and decided to stay in. So instead of staying in, I tagged along with my real family. Now I think at this point is where all the trouble started.

Now if, you remember, I told you that my families are like night and day. My real family takes trips every year so the kids

44

can have a vacation before returning to school. So their trips are always kid friendly, no matter where they go. The kids are always given enough spending money, to make sure that they can have lots of fun. So when I tagged along, and they realized that I didn't have any money, they were completely shocked but paid for everything.

When I returned to the hotel with all of my things, I could tell that my foster mother was a little angry. The next day, when similar things began to happen, such as the places that my real family had chosen for us to eat, I guess the choices that were made were not too cool. And for the first time I started to hear my foster mom say some negative things about my real family.

So upon returning to the hotel, just like thieves in the night, we left my real family sleeping in their rooms and headed for home in the middle of the night.

Family Loyalty
January 1990 (Age 16)

Well it seems like everything has gone haywire since finding my real family. My foster mom and I barely get along; as a matter of fact we are more like enemies. She does not like my family very much, especially my great auntie. She says "that they smelling their own shit, but don't think it stinks." Oh! And my favorite, "I am spoiled, and they have tainted me." I think that she is just a little jealous of the way that they treat me. I have learned so much since hanging around them, such as... how you are supposed to treat a human being! I feel like my foster mom had her chance to be just like them, to treat me like I was her real daughter (all the time), and I should have never been reminded that I was a foster kid, with her or any family.

Don't get me wrong, things here aren't always bad. But I do feel that if I was born with my foster family's blood running through my veins, I would have been treated much differently and the rules would not be the same.

Things have become so unbearable around here. The other day she accused me of "having my nose turned up," ever since I found my family. I even get into it with her daughter, and we used to be so cool. Now they are both so mad at me that they stopped doing anything for me. I am a mess and things are going downhill. All I do is work, go to school, and get fussed at for something every single day! My life right now is so confusing. I have no one to talk to, I feel like I am playing tug-a-war with both families. If I had to describe it, it would be a giant mud puddle placed in the middle of a tug-a-war game, and the family that falls in first, that's the family I don't gain. But for now, I just push forward, because I still want to build this relationship with my real family.

And The Winner Is
March 1990 (Age16)

Guess what?!! I am finally out of here! Last night I got into this huge argument with my foster mother and her daughter. I came home from work, Yes that's right! I am still working and in school! I work late nights, sometimes getting home at 1am, and I still manage to make it to school every day and on time! When I walked in from work last night, everyone was sitting in the dining room (my foster mom, her husband, her daughter and three new foster sisters), helping my foster mom with something. I said hello when I walked in the door at 12:30am and not one person responded. So I just shook my head and started up the stairs to my bedroom. I was tired; I don't even think I put a toe across my bedroom doorway, when my foster mom and foster sister (her daughter), started fussing at me. They wanted me to come downstairs, to help with some project that everyone was working on. Although extremely tired, I managed to make it back downstairs to begin working with them. And that's when they started in on me. Both my foster mom and her daughter started telling me that I was lazy and disrespectful, among other things. So at that moment, I felt like I began to twitch and steam started coming out of my ears, and I just snapped!

I went off, completely losing my mind! I began yelling and cussing and telling them that they never did care about me! I told my foster mom "respect can be given, but you also have to respect me!" I told her that was tired of coming to this house and nobody speaks to me! I was tired of working to support myself to receive the littlest things! I was tired of walking on egg shells trying to keep the peace! I was tired of her talking about my family! I even told her that I knew she was in it for the money! After all of that, my foster sister (her daughter) looked at me and said, "Who in the hell do you think you're talking to?"

Honestly, until the recent chain of events her daughter and I have always gotten along, so I had never seen her that mad at me before. So at that moment I thought to myself, she is going to kill me, if nothing else. I was so mad and scared all at the same time, but I swear to you fear became my strength! Since I have been here, I have never stood up for myself for anything. So for the first time I really did not care or was not cautious before I opened my mouth to speak!

My foster mom and her daughter were furious, and both stood there the color of bright red. Next thing I know, I am back upstairs, and in my room with my foster mom's husband trying to breaking up the mutiny. As they all left my room, my foster mother turned and said, "You gotta get the hell out of my house before someone ends up dead." This was her way of saying my time had expired from being in her house and that I had to leave. I thought to myself finally I am free!

I am FREE
May *1990* (Age16)

I can not believe it! I am writing in this journal while sitting in my new bedroom, in a new house! Yep that is right I am finally free! Approximately four days after that explosion in my foster mom's house, I moved in with my dad and my family! So I now live with my real family (also known as my Biological Family). I have been here almost two months, and I am amazed at how quickly my life has changed. I now live with my dad, his wife, my brother, and my little sister, who comes to visit every other week. I feel so free! I still have my own room, but with a much bigger bed. I also get to go to the grocery store and pick out my own food, instead of eating what someone else may have a taste for. It is like a breath of fresh air!

My dad works the night shift, so he is only here in the daytime, and for some of that time he is either gone or asleep. But that does not bother me, I have his wife, my brother and my sister, and that is OK by me! My dad's wife and I are always buying clothes or going out shopping; she even taught me how to do my own hair, this way I won't have to spend as much money at the salon, every week. I can now do my own perms for free! My brother and I get along like two peas in a pod. He's my stepbrother, but in my family we don't say step or half of anything. So basically he is my brother and nothing in between. He's one year older than me and has a music studio in his room, so we are always fooling around making music and beats. Then comes my little sister, she is much younger than me, but I really enjoy her company. When she visits we play video games and watch movies.

As for my appearance, it has totally changed! I now wear contact lenses, no more thick glasses for me. I also dress a lot nicer, because my wardrobe does not depend upon, what thrift store I go to, or my own money. Now when I go shopping, I come back with too many things. It's funny when I stop to think about it, Ms. Lawson (my foster mother) went from buying me some things, to buying me a few things, to eventually buying me nothing. But I don't have that problem here. On top of that, I still have my job, but with way less hours, my dad wants me to concentrate fully on school and just being a teen. This is a perfect place for me!

These two pictures I found neatly tucked away in my journal. On the far left is a picture of my brother and me, standing outside the apartment that we both shared, with my father, my stepmom, and my little sister. To the far right is my little sister.
(I love you guys and thank you for allowing me to share this)

Chapter 5 – Not So Family After All

I always got me ^(poem written age17)

You may not have a family that will love you until the end
You must love yourself like you're your own best friend.
It may not be what you want
But for right now it is all that you need.
Because at the end of the day ME is all I can conceive.

Not even settled yet
August 1990 ^(Age17)

Well I have been here almost five months, and things started out great, but it is not what you think. I am still being treated well, and everything here is gravy. It's my parents! They argue all the time, when they think we are asleep. I never hear what the arguments are about, but I can't help to feel that the arguments are about me. I mean I did enter into their perfect little world, not to mention that I am another mouth to feed. I confronted my brother about the arguments and apparently this is something that he is used to. Well, I hope they stop arguing and work everything out real soon, because school is about to start and I do not need any negativity floating around me, especially while I am in school.

The Fall of 1990 ^(Age17)

Well it has been crazy around here, we all found out what the arguing was all about. It had nothing to do with me! Long before my arrival my parents' marriage was falling apart (thank God it wasn't me). They are getting a divorce, and my dad and I are moving. As quick as I got here, the faster I have to leave. So now we are moving back to my old neighborhood (perfect for me). I will miss my brother and new mother, it has been decided that my brother will remain with his mother and I will still see my little sister every other week.

So now I am sitting here thinking about "the life that I call me." I always say that phrase when things start off good but end up bad or crazy. It seems like this type of life will always be a part of me.

Growing up to fast
November 1990 (Age17)

Well, we moved into our new house and it is all right. This part of my old neighborhood is not considered "the good part," but I guess it will have to do. Living with my dad is not what I expected. So far he is rarely at home, but when he is here, he is either sleeping or entertaining (if you know what I mean). My grandpa and great aunt call and checks in on me, every day. Through these phone calls and other things, I learned that my great aunt calls all the shots in this family, pretty much what she says goes, and that's how it's going to be.

I wish things could go back to the way they use to be. So far I went from having it all, from a "TV made family," to losing it all and being left feeling sad and empty. Today I realized that in the course of almost eight months, I have moved twice and lost a whole family. Nonetheless, life has to move on. So far living with my dad, on our own, has been a little fun and interesting. My dad allowed me to have a few parties, inviting all my friends from school and people on my street. He also taught me how to tie a tie, so now I borrow all his ties and suit jackets to wear to school (he hates it when I do). I even talked my dad into buying some cool jeans and finally getting a "in style" hair cut (but that didn't last long).

Even with the good times here, things are still not what I am used to. I always feel like I live by myself because I have so much free reign. I basically come and go as I please. The only thing I have to do is leave a note somewhere for my dad to see. I keep the house clean and try to cook what I can, but mostly we eat fast food (but that's cool). We don't even have a washing machine or dryer. Therefore, I'm stuck going over to my grandpa's or to my great aunt's house to wash clothes, rotating every other week. I know that my dad works nights to provide for me, but I feel neglected and very lonely. So I started having company all hours of the night, so I can feel protected and safe.

I even miss Ms. Lawson, and her family. There, I had some home cooked meals (even if it had to be a big pot of something, that usually lasted a week). I even miss the laughter at night from my foster sisters running around playing with me. Hell, I even miss the dog, playing with him and walking him down the street. I am just saying, living here is starting to make me completely unhappy.

Sex, A Boyfriend and Not Me
November 1990 (Age17)

I came home today, and my dad's car was in the driveway for a change. As soon as I entered the house I heard the sounds of a female screaming, from what one would call "the pleasure of sex." I wouldn't even know that pleasure, even though I lost my virginity last year at 16 to my boyfriend and let me tell you, it was not that pleasurable. It was hot, it hurt like hell and I threw up afterwards. So I still do not see a valid reason for doing it. I mean yea, it's suppose to be a form of affection, to show someone that you love them, but as far as I am concerned they can keep that! As for my dad I understand that he is a grown ass man, <u>BUT</u> his "stanky" female friend don't even have respect for me. What kind of woman sleeps around with a man, while a kid is in the house? I'll tell you "stanky." The sad thing about all of this is that, I bet my dad does not realize how disrespectful this is to me. Damn he knows what time I get out of school, why couldn't they have just wrapped it up sooner, just "stanky."

But hey, I am not going to let that get me down; because later today the house will be empty as usual, and my boyfriend will be home from college, for the holiday. I can not wait for him to get here. When he is home he gives me a break from the madness of my reality. He reminds me that nothing in this world matters except me! I love it when he comes home, we hang out, go to the movies, shoot pool, you name it, we do just about everything. When I hang out with him, I just feel so comfortable and free. He says that when I turn 18, he is going to take me away from here so I can be happy.

Time Heals Old Wounds
December 1990 (Age17)

Guess what Ms. Lawson and I are speaking. I saw her in the store and we have been talking on the phone ever since. I even stop by her house every day after school. I hang out with my foster sisters, and believe it or not even her daughter and I are back cool. My foster mom has been real nice, and I am actually having a lot of fun at her house. Sometimes I even spend the night over there; and when she heard about how I have to wash my clothes by switching houses every other week, she began washing some of my clothes for me. It sounds crazy, but through everything that my foster mom and I have been through, visiting with her has been like a breath of fresh air to me.

To Grandpa's House We Go
December 1990 (Age17)

Well we are moving again, this time into my grandpa's house (move number three), because according to my family, "I have been acting kind of wild and crazy." Well, let's see: I ran up a thousand dollar phone bill talking to my boyfriend, who is away at college. I took all my clothes to my foster mother's house with plans of running away. Apparently according to my great aunt, "I am out of control" so we had to move. She said that someone has to keep an eye on me. Correct me if I am wrong, but isn't that my dad's responsibility? The reality of my situation just amazes me. If my family would just take a look at the bigger picture, they could see that I never really had a time to adjust to moving around, new rules and let's face it, I am still getting to know them too!

Everything in my life is so messed up, some days I can't even think straight. Maybe trying to become a part of my biological family was not such a great idea. I don't fit in with them, I feel as if I am watching scenes from a play and every now and then, the audience (me) gets a chance to participate. "I don't belong here, I don't belong anywhere."

Living with Grandpa
January 1991 (Age17)

Things here at grandpa's house seem to be real cool. Grandpa keeps the freezer supplied with my favorite frozen pizza and every chance I get I ask him to play spoons (it's a fun card game he taught me). I still have my own room, my uncle lives here to (we are the same age), and well my dad...I see him every now and then because he still works nights or he is gone bowling once or twice a week. Although I don't want to be here, at least I have someone in the house with me every night and I am getting home cooked meals. So I guess you could say, "that's the brighter side of things."

Just Rest In Peace Dear Mother
January 1991 (Age17)

I received a phone call today that will be forever branded in my mind. I was told today that my first foster mother has died. The terrible news was delivered by my first set of foster sisters, and all I could do was cry. I can't believe that this has happened, and she's gone! I just found my first foster family a few months ago, but have not physically seen them in years. I can honestly say: "that the love I have in my heart for them has never died." I will never forget the fact that I lived with them for many years, completely unaware that I was even a foster child. Right now I am so angry because she meant the world to me!

I was taken away from her and now look at me! I understand that she was getting sick, but look how the agency has treated me. Allowing me to be thrown around like a rag doll, not to mention I come with a monthly fee. Who treats kids that way? Just take you from your family and toss you to total strangers and expect you to smile, accept it, be quiet and act pretty!
Did those social workers even stop to think of the hurt or pain that it would cause me? I just know in my heart the agency could have removed me differently, I mean come on....bribing me with my own room, Disney World and frequent visits to the movies! Hell, I couldn't even tell you what Disney World looks like to this day! They just took me away and expected me to go "cold turkey," as if I was detoxing from a drug or something. I was cut off from them, no phone calls, visits, NOTHING! My mother (I

56

still call my first foster mom that) was just sick, not abusive to me.

Now my mother is gone, and all I have left of her is my memories...I remember cooking in the kitchen, laughing with my mother, and making up silly recipes. I can even remember her rocking me to sleep countless of nights, from being scared out of my mind, from having the same scary dream. My sisters were there for me too, taking me to school, the park, the mall, and even to the movies. It's funny but I can even recall dressing like them, I remember us wearing matching outfits, as we walked down the street.

Right now I am totally numb, I am sitting here with tears streaming down my face and my heart feeling as if it weighed a ton. Today is the worst day ever and what can I do about it NOTHING...

This picture was given to me by my sisters (seen above), all of us together (my first foster family). My mom is holding the baby (my nephew), and of course me, (far left). Every year we took a family portrait, but due to unforeseen events, this may be the only family portrait left in existence.

(I love you guys and thank you for allowing me to share this)

The Lock Down
February 1991 ^(Age17)

It's been a month since my mom died, I feel a little better since the last time I wrote in here. I had a chance to go to the funeral, and I was included in everything, from the family car, to the obituary (which listed me as one of her daughters). She may be gone but, I do feel better because I know that she is no longer sick and at peace.

As for me, I am still at Grandpa's house, and things started off fine, but now it's kind of rocky. Things are beginning to fall apart. I was slowly put on "lock down," because grandpa doesn't want me to be "wild." I can't talk on the phone long, I can't go out much and my curfew is extremely early. I even had to quit my job at the restaurant, where my tips were "gravy!" So now I work with my uncle at the mall, shoveling popcorn at a damn popcorn shop, and even that job was arranged by the family. I guess I now live in a dictatorship, with the only thing missing is my grandpa telling me how to walk, talk and brush my damn teeth. At this point, I am suffocating here. I wish I never left Ms. Lawson's house, at least there I was free. Maybe things there weren't as bad as it seemed; I talk to her just about every day and believe it or not she says the same thing, "she wished I never left." I wish that I could get far away from here and be at peace.

Interruption from the author for current or former foster kids:
All I ever wanted was to find my biological family and to reunite with them, and when that happened my happiness was only temporary. I thought that things would be great, and I would fit right in. Boy was I wrong! I was so excited with the idea of "family," that I did not take the time to get to know them and for them to get to know me. I still needed to heal from a life of

resentment and my feelings of abandonment and pain. The hardest part for me was accepting the fact that I did not get along with all of my family members, and that moving back home may not have been the best choice for me. So, if I had it to do all over again or to give any advice it would be this: Take YOUR time and work through a healing process with your biological family. This would include getting to know each other. Please understand that this process is not going to happen overnight (seek professional help or have a support person in place, if necessary). Most importantly move at your own pace and remember to set your boundaries and personal rules. Lastly, keep in mind that as much as you may want to be re-connected with your family, these things take time, and the end result may or may not be the one that you are looking for. If that happens, you have to relax, regroup and restart your thought process; and most importantly stay positive and surround yourself with positive people and positive things!

This was a drawing that was tucked away in my journal between March & April of 1991

I recall drawing this picture and remember being extremely sad at the time. I remember having no one to talk to, so I began to draw and this picture was the end result.

Back Where I Belong

March 1991 (Age17)

I moved back into my old foster home today (the Lawsons'). This was the best move for me, although deep in my heart, I wish that things would have worked out with my biological family. But I must move forward, not to mention that I am so glad to be back in my comfort zone; free from all the bio-family drama and negativity. As of today, I am on a positive road trying to put the twisted pieces of my life back together again.

Before I left here, I was walking down a path of greatness especially at school: I was graduating an entire year early, a member of two organizations including President and Founder of my own student organization, in the gospel choir, and a student community liaison. Now look at me: struggling to catch up to graduate on time; my organization that I was so proud of has damn near disbanded; and I am nobody's community liaison! It is amazing what stress can do, when you are surrounded by constant negative drama. I am so looking forward to getting myself together.

On a positive note, I am settling back in nicely. I now have five foster sisters, and I share a room with three of them. It's cool because it feels like I never left, we used to hang out a lot even before I officially moved back in, so the room arrangement is perfect.

The Good One The Outcast and Me

April 1991 (Age17)

Well I have been back for over a month now. Things are still running smoothly. I have not had any major issues. On the other hand, my foster sisters have been in and out of trouble, so I am considered "the good one," for now. We all tend to switch roles weekly. Last week I was "the outcast," which basically means I did something wrong (God only knows what), most of the time I have no idea why I am being labeled "the outcast of the week." Basically this is how it works: when I am "the outcast," I get treated differently than the other girls for about a week. For example, the "good one" may get a chance to go out to a restaurant, stay out past the 9pm curfew etc, while "the outcast" will not get a chance to do anything and will be talked about negatively all week.

The sad part about all of this is that "the good one," without even realizing it begins to treat "the outcast" mean. This outcast thing has always been a common occurrence in this household even before I left. It's almost like some freaky science experiment, but it's okay and I know that I can handle it. The real problem is that it sometimes causes jealousy issues between us girls, but we have recently banded together to try our best to prevent this from happening. I think foster parents should treat everyone in the house the same, hell it's not our fault that we are here.

A Positive Future...Maybe
April 1991 (Age17)

On a more positive note, things at school are looking a whole lot brighter; my grades are rising, while I prepare to play catch up in summer school. Not to mention I got my old job back waitressing! Right now, everything is looking positive for me. I am still dating my boyfriend; he left college and has now joined the military. We keep in contact by letters, and he calls once a week. We have spent so much time apart over this last year, so being apart has become the norm for me. My friends wonder why I even bother trying to hold on to him, especially since we can't see each other like normal couples.

I know it's weird, but I don't even know if I love him or if he genuinely loves me. All I know is that he has stood by me, when no one else would. Not to mention he was my first. He talks about marriage a lot and how he wants to take me away from all this negativity. Marriage to me means being whisked away from here on a white horse…or better yet being carried to safety by an angel with wings, that is what marriage means to me. But for now I am stuck in this hellish reality, trying to stay on a positive path that unwinds the twisted pieces of me.

A Social Worker's Business
May 1991 (Age17)

My social worker came by my house today. He is a young guy and fine! You should see my house every time he comes to visit, the girls in the house turn into animals at the zoo. Whether he is on a visit or just picking me up, for something afterschool, all the girls in the house try to hang out in the kitchen, so they can get a peek. I'll admit at first when he became my social worker, I was like well damn did the Agency run out of adults? But I quickly learned that he is grown and "he don't play." He may look way too young to be a social worker, but he gets straight down to business.

If I am acting a fool, he is there laying down the foster care law. Whenever there is an issue in school, he is on it. If I got a problem at the house he is there. Although, sometimes there are issues going on that I dare not discuss, for fear of being removed. But honestly, I think if he knew those issues, he would try to tackle that too.

It's funny because when he first started coming around, I wouldn't say much. I would just sit there and act mean and rude. Sometimes, I would bring my crocheting needles and yarn, and rudely crochet while he talked to me. Until one day, he asked me about my crocheting.

I think I probably stared at him as if he was crazy, all while thinking to myself, he is 6 feet tall, married (yea I know ladies), and built like a pro-athlete...hmmm...I really don't think he gives a rat's ass, about crocheting. BUT, I was very surprised that a social worker was asking me something about me.

He wasn't barking orders, or throwing foster care rules and terms down my throat, or even fussing at me for something I did or didn't do. He wasn't reading me a list of things I gotta do, or my favorite...asking me that same stupid ass question, "How are you doing?" On a side note, let me rant about that: I find that question so annoying, "How are you doing?" I want to say so bad, "How in the hell do you think I'm doing?" and "Didn't you read that mile and a half long file on me?" Anyway, as bad as I want to say it, I don't. I usually say that I am "fine" or "okay."

Okay I am done with my rant...back to the crocheting thing. On that day our visit was different, all because he was not shoveling foster care rules down my throat or any other foster care related thing. He was interested in me, and one of my favorite hobbies, crocheting. He asked about other things I like to do, and I think from that day forward, I was little nicer to him. I consider him one of the best social workers that I have had so far.

It's Not the 4th of July
But I must prepare for my Independence Day
May 1991 (Age17)

When my social worker was here the other day, he signed me up for these life skills classes, "Independent Living." He said that these classes will be helpful for me when I become independent and will no longer be in foster care. So now two Saturdays out of the month, I will be in life skills training. How boring! I will be sitting in a classroom with other foster kids, learning about banking (I already have a bank account), job skills (HELLO, I have been working since I was 14), budgeting and a whole bunch of other classes. How irritating! Who wants to catch a bus on a Saturday to go sit in some class. Not me! And why in the hell are they teaching me this stuff now? I am 17 about to be grown…A little late don't you think? Well, anyway I am starting this Saturday.

An Irritating Saturday
May 1991 (Age17)

It's Saturday, and I have already wasted my morning, so I will make today's entry short. I went to those so-call "Life skills" or "Independent Living" classes. One word, BORING!! All you do is sit in a classroom, with a bunch of other foster kids who act up and complain, (because they don't want to be there either), while a teacher bores the hell out of you with paperwork, chalk board writings and rules! Don't they realize we get that in school? Where is the fun? Can't we play some fun games? What a waste of my two Saturdays! The only reason that I am coming back here is for the free bus tickets and the free food!

Just Thinking About 18
May 1991 (Age17)

It's crazy being back here. Some mornings I just wake up and stare at the ceiling, thinking about all of the things in my 17 years that I have been through. I will be grown next month, turning the big 18! But I won't be leaving foster care just yet because I haven't graduated from school. 18, what does that really mean? My social worker talks a lot about how my independence is important and that I must take those "Independent Living" classes seriously. I waited so long for this moment so I could be "out of here," but to be honest now I am just scared. I have been so busy all these years searching for peace that I feel I am so far behind in my thinking, such as, what will I do after high school? Am I going to college? Where will I be? Right now I am so disconnected from any type of reality. I mean, I don't talk to my real family and connecting with them ended in disaster. Even my foster mom says that I need to be thinking about what I am going to do soon. So I doubt if I can stay here. Maybe turning 18, is not so great.

Birthdays Mean Nothing to Me
June 1991 (Age18)

Today is my 18th birthday and it's just another day closer to me leaving foster care. My social worker sent me a birthday card, he is only the second worker to do that in my long foster care history. The card had 20 bucks in it, so I thought that was pretty cool. But I can't spend it because I have to save up to get ready to move. You would think that I would be happy today, out celebrating early and acting a fool; but I am not, all I can think about is, soon I will have to move. Most kids my age are out with their families having fun, preparing to have a perfect senior year or even by now away at college. Not me, all I can think about is my life, turning 18 and eventually being out on my own.

I know today won't be all miserable, I will be hanging out with a few friends; not to mention I will eventually end up at my best friend's house eating up all her food. I spend a lot time there, on the weekends and after school. I am over there so much, that now her mom leaves a plate in the oven for both of us after school. So I know today will get better.

The Proposal
June 1991 (Age18)

I am ENGAGED!! I have a diamond ring and everything! My boyfriend...I mean Fiancé!! Just asked me to marry him today! He had the whole thing planned out for weeks. For starters he tricked me, all week long he kept telling me that he was not coming home for his military break. He made up some excuse about going on vacation with his mother. So I had been upset all week long, until today, when he showed up at my doorstep, and surprised the heck out of me. I was so happy to see him that I nearly knocked him over when I opened the door.

We hung out all day. We went to the movies, out to dinner and then stopped off at the park in my neighborhood. None of this was unusual because we always did those things. BUT, at the park we threw the ball around for awhile, got a drink of water and sat down on the bench. That's when he looked at me and told me that, he might be going away to live in another country. Now I will tell you, right then and there, I think my heart stopped. The tears instantly began to fall, and on top of that I was angry. I just started to cry harder and harder, I mean almost like a newborn baby. I got up from that bench and started to

68

leave. He got up right behind me, yelling at me, asking me to wait and to hear him out. After he calmed me down, we sat back on the bench.

At this point, I honestly didn't have anything to say, so I just sat there staring at him, with the meanest look ever (I wish I had a mirror to see it). He told me that he loved me and that he made a promise to me that he would never leave. At this point, he is in front of the bench, staring at me and all in my face; but I am so mad that I don't even notice that he is down on one knee. He continues on to say, "I want you to come with me so I can take care of you." Then out comes this small, black velvet box. He opened the box and just like that he said, "I love you, will you marry me." I jumped up from that bench and screamed as loud as I could "YES!!" We were hugging and kissing, I know the people on the basketball court, thought we were downright crazy!

Words can not express the way that I feel right now. I am finally going to get away from here! I am finally going to leave all my troubles behind. I am finally going to be FREE! No more social works, agencies, foster care, I can finally be at peace.

Summer Fun and Some Good Eats
June 1991 (Age18)

I am 18, engaged, on summer break and on vacation from my job for the next two weeks! Then summer school will be starting and then it's back to the books. In the meantime, I am determined to have a little fun. My fiancé is stuck in some military training camp and expecting me to write him every week; he must be crazy, not me in this 90 degree heat. I am not sitting in nobody's hot house, writing a damn letter. I am out of here! I am about to hit the streets!

69

I think I will head over to a few of my friends houses, so I can get something tasty to eat. I am so sick of spaghetti, chicken, chili, greens and stew. If you are wondering why, it's a long running joke among the girls in the house, because those are our monthly selections for rotating meals (excluding holidays). We think it's because it's so many of us, she has to cook enough for everybody and to make it last an entire week. So I usually eat at a friend's house, work or get some fast food; either way I'm happy.

Engagement Blues
July 1991 (Age18)

Well, I have been back four months and so far, so good. Nothing out of the unusual except my foster mother thinks that I am too young to get married. She thinks that I am making a terrible mistake. She even had the nerve to ask me, was I pregnant (she must be crazy). A baby, that is the last thing on my mind, I can barely take care of me. She even asked for my fiancé's mom's number so she could call to see if she approved of the marriage. I gave it to her, because as far as I know his mother likes me.

Now my cousin (who visits every summer) and foster sisters have joined in, on torturing me. Teasing me about my ring, saying things like, "it's so small that we can hardly see it." I even heard, "you can't even cook, so your husband is going to starve." The list just goes on and on. Yea, it's hurtful, but soon I will be sitting pretty, in my house, in a whole other country; away from everyone. They can all laugh and talk about me now, but soon it will be me, my husband and the military. Where will they be, sitting here in foster care and wishing they were free!

70

The Master Plan
September 1991 (Age18)

Well, I am about to embark on my senior year of high school. Class of 1992, oddly enough I will have completed all of my graduation credits this December 1991, but because my high school does not have mid-quarter graduations, I can't walk across stage until summer, 1992. It's cool all, of my friends are in the class of 1992 anyway (except a few).

So far I have not signed up for too many school activities, but I am on the drill team and in the gospel choir, and I think that's enough for me. It's my senior year, so I want to enjoy everything. My fiancé and I have been discussing a lot of things, like homecoming, prom and other social activities. He knows that he won't be able to escort me, because of his military duties.

So we came up with a plan, on who can take me and how it should be done. If we know in advance who I have chosen to escort me to a school event, then that person will meet him if he is home on leave. If he is not home from the military on leave, then I have to set up a three-way phone conversation with that person, myself and him. Now I think, this is only fair, after all I am his wife to be.

I Just Want To be Happy
October 1991 (Age18)

Well, I have been here seven months, and I can not understand why God can't hear me. I pray for peace, I ask for forgiveness but in return, nothing. Ever since I got engaged my foster mother has turned my happiness into frustration and agony.

I am convinced that she really does not want to see me get married. Right now I am so stressed out! I ask myself every day, why can't I just be happy? My foster mom is driving crazy, with this whole marriage thing. She really needs to stay out of my business and stop interfering. She constantly reminds me that, "she's going to make me honor that ring." Like I'm cheating, I am faithful, and she has no idea what she is talking about. I haven't cheated on my fiancé, but according to her, "she knows everything." She has been fussing at me all day, talking about how she is going to tell him everything! Now I am thinking to myself, tell him what? I talk to him twice a week, so he knows just about everything.

As she's yelling at me, she goes on to say how, "I am wrong for going to homecoming with another guy and hanging out in the streets." I could not believe what I was hearing…all of this yelling and cussing over homecoming. If she would have just taken the time to actually talk to me, she might find out that, "things are not always what they seem." My fiancé knows all about Troy, the guy that I took to homecoming. They spoke to each other by three-way a few weeks ago and he was granted permission to escort me. All I know is that I just want to be happy!

I swear ever since this engagement, things around here are absolutely crazy! My foster mother treats me as if I am her enemy. I have to do everything for myself and she stopped including me in household planned activities. For example, sometimes I would come home and the house would be empty, but when everyone did come home, they would return with restaurant boxes and shopping bags. "Like I don't want to shop or eat!" I ask myself all the time, "What is the cost of true happiness?" Because, whatever it costs, I will gladly pay the fee! I just want to be happy!

The Insane Letter

This absolutely insane and I am going to go crazy! I just need to get away from here! I received a disturbing letter from my fiancé today. He writes me once a week, and his letters are always uplifting and mushy (which I like). But this letter was a little different, this one made my heart feel betrayed and heavy. It starts off like this:

Dear My Love and Only,
I just got back from my "marriage in the military class," so you know that I was thinking about you. I love you so much and I don't want to lose you. I know that I left you, to fight an uphill battle alone, and for that, I am truly sorry. So when you read this letter, please don't get into a fight with your foster mother.

Now right then and there, I knew that something was wrong! The letter then goes on to say:

Your foster mother has been plotting to destroy our relationship, from the start and now she has gone too far. I received a letter from my grandmother today, and I talked to my mother this week. According to my grandmother and my mother, I am a fool. Your foster mother has been secretly talking to my mother about you and it has not been good. For Starters, I don't have time to tell you everything, so I will only highlight a few:

- *You have multiple boyfriends*
- *You are a party girl*
- *The only reason you moved from your real family is because you ran up a $1000 dollar phone bill*

- *Your grades are terrible*
- *You can't even get a grant or a scholarship*
- *You're not getting into any college*

I mean the list just goes on and on! Why would your foster mother do such a horrible thing? Now I have to tell you at first I was really mad, but I realize that I trust and love you, and I know in my heart that these things couldn't possibly be true! I love you and want to marry you. But I need you to be good, and do good for us. I am handling the rest from here. I gotta go, I miss you and I will be home soon.

Oh! My God!! WHY? The tears have been streaming down my face, and I just can not stop screaming in my pillow, my voice sounds cracked and chafed, almost to a silent whisper, one that I can not escape. WHY? Why would she do this to me? She just refuses to let me be happy! I don't have multiple boyfriends, I am not a party girl, and I am actually getting out of school a whole semester early! She has no idea of who I am, or what I stand for, she knows absolutely nothing. Why won't she accept me being happy? What is it about me that she does not like? I will get married, I will move far away, I will be happy, I will be free.

The Déjà vu of November 1991
December 1991 (Age18)

ENOUGH! I just could not take it no more! My fiancé is home on leave. Now you would think that this would be a happy journal entry, one filled with love and joy...NOT.

While visiting his mother a few days ago, she confronted me and my fiancé, about all lies, and unfounded evidence that my foster mother had filled her head with. I just sat there and cried as she went off on me. She told me that I was no good for her son, and how I have his head in the clouds "with this marriage thing." She even went on to say that her son was a fool for getting mixed up with me, and that I am "a liar and a cheat." Then she looked at my fiancé, who had been sitting there saying absolutely nothing and asked him, "Did you know that she went to homecoming?" Now this was my fiancé's big shining moment to stand up me, but guess what I got, absolutely NOTHING!! He just sat there staring off into space, even though he knew all about the homecoming thing. His mother told me that I better get it together if I wanted to continue to be with her son. I left there angry, hurt and confused. Why didn't my fiancé say something? I was too upset to confront him with anything! So you know, when I got home it was on!

First I talked to one of my foster sisters in the house, who coincidentally knew everything. She said that my foster mother had been talking bad about me to my fiancé's mother for months. My foster sister said that she just did not want to say anything, for fear of being "the outcast" (go figure). After that, I went off on my foster mother about everything!

She was standing in the kitchen, and the questions and accusations just begin to fly out my mouth. I point blank asked her, "How does it feel to treat a person less than a human being?" And with that it was on. I confronted her about all of the lies that she had told to my fiancé's family about me. I was crying and screaming, all while she was cussing me out. But I did not care, I asked another question, "Why don't you want to see me happy?" She never answered that question. But she did manage to call me a few choice words while telling me "to get the hell out of her sight!"

At this point, I could see all of my foster sisters peeking from the stairs as if they had a front row seat to a boxing match, that was long overdue. I was so angry, that I ran past them crying, up the stairs and into my room. I grabbed as much as I could and shoved it into my backpack, and headed out the front door. I had no idea where I was going or what I was going to do. When I got to the corner of my street, I headed to the nearest payphone and called my fiancé. He told me to stay where I was and that he was coming back to get me.

So now, I have not been home for two days. I stayed in a hotel one night and at my best friend's house the next night. I did call home, to tell her where I was, and all she said, was "from now on, she does not give a damn what I do, because come June she is through!" and she slammed down the phone.

I am so tired of fighting my way through my life, just to find happiness and peace. I thought coming back here, was a smart move, and that myself, my foster mother and our relationship had matured, but I was wrong...coming back here has been nothing but Déjà vu.

My fiancé used to write me once a week, while he was away in the military. I found some of these old letters, hidden in between the pages of one of my journals. Not only were they interesting to read, but they were also cool to see, so I decided to share a picture of them with you. (Note: the envelope's address was removed due to privacy)

Chapter 7 – Twisted But Not Free

Twisted *(Poem)*

Unravel my mind from this innocent reality

Pull apart my soul from this unfaithful misery

Sacrifice my heart for this untold insanity

Am I Twisted

Take a hold of this road for the childhood of humanity

Rip apart my vision so my sight won't be mad at me

Wisdom so clear but the world just laughs at me

Am I Twisted

My heart in your hands cause it just won't beat for me

Air is so clear but it just won't breathe for me

Legs wanna run but not enough speed in me

Am I Twisted

Searching for happiness but can't seem to keep it

Hungry in my mind but life declines to feed it

Energy is gone restless and defeated

Am I Twisted

A Fool-Proof Plan

January 1992 (Age18)

Well, it's been a little over a month since the big blowout at home. So much has changed: for starters, I am finished with high school; I finished an entire semester early (like I told everyone I would). Now I am just waiting for the graduation to take place in June. As for my foster mother, she barely speaks to me. So for now I am pretty much on my own.

I pretty much come and go as I please. My foster mother was serious when she said, "from now on I don't give a damn what you do." So I have designed a method in order to "keep the peace" and to quietly stay out of her way. Some days I stay at my best friend's house or work double shifts waitressing. On my off days, when I have nowhere to go, or nothing to do, I sneak back up to the high school, and eat lunch with my friends. Finally on the days when I have no options, for example maybe I can't go over my best friend's house, I just stay in my room all day. So far this method has been a fool-proof plan.

Not So Happily

January 1992 (Age18)

I have not spoken to my fiancé this week. He doesn't have to write me as much anymore because he has gained complete phone privileges. We still talk about marriage and the houses on the base. But to tell you the truth, I don't know if I want to be married. It's not because I don't love him, it's just ever since the blowout in December, things just don't seem right to me. I am trying not to hold on to the chain of events in my mind, but I can't help but think…Why wouldn't he stand up for me? Why didn't he defend me? Where was the help I so desperately needed? There I was all alone, cornered by all of that negativity, and he did nothing to protect me, even though he knew the truth.

Every time I think about it, it just brings me to tears. I think about it every day. I ask myself, is this how it's going to be? I get married, move to some foreign land or even another state, and he won't be there to protect me. Right now, the thought of marriage does not make me happy.

My Best Friend
February 1992 (Age18)

Well, things around here have been pretty quiet. I have actually been having fun for a change. My best friend and I have been "hanging tough." We go to the movies, bowling, or just hanging out at the mall it really doesn't matter. I am having so much fun hanging with her. When I hang out with her, or her family, I forget my own terrible reality. I even call her mother "mom," and believe it or not my best friend or her mom would not have it any other way. As a matter of fact, they tell me all the time, "you are a part of our family." Honestly, if it weren't for my best friend and her family, I don't know where I would be half of the time. So I am always excited when we hang out because I know that we are going to embark onto some weekend wild adventure, that we probably can never speak about. I am so glad I met her, she came into my life right on time. We laugh together, cry together, and for that I am truly grateful. Truth be told, she has the perfect family, her mom and family always look out for her, and she never "wants for anything." My best friend is very lucky, and I am so glad that she accepts me for me, and does not mind sharing me with her family.

Sexual Escapes
February 1992 (Age18)

Last night, my fiancé and I stayed at a hotel (like we often do), having a night of what I like to call "a sexual escape." A sexual escape is when you just have sex, to please the other person you're dating; and you shut down and take your mind to some paradise or calming beach, until having sex is through. I have sexual escapes, just to keep him happy and my life peaceful.

During my sexual escapes, I picture myself riding in a red car, top down, luggage in the back and getting far away from here. Sometimes, I imagine myself going on an adventure sipping ice tea, in the land of paradise. Truth be told I don't like "sexual escapes." The escape part is cool, but the sex part just seems so unnecessary. But I know that if I stop or refuse, I will lose him and my way out of this nightmare. I hate it and it sucks, but what else am I supposed to do? To make things worse, last night our time together felt different, I felt different, I felt like I escaped to a dungeon and there was no paradise, just a hollow shell, there was no adventure, I felt completely empty. And I don't know why.

The Truth Shall Set You Free
February 1992 (Age18)

I am sitting here on my bed, eyes red, with endless tears streaming down my face. The hurt and the pain that I feel can never be erased. I just found out that my fiancé has been cheating on me.

It all started when we were at the hotel, I asked him for a couple of dollars, to help me out for the week. His response was "sure just look in my wallet and get what you need." He then walked into the bathroom and started taking a shower. I opened his wallet, grabbed twenty bucks and there it was, damn near in plain sight. There it was me staring at it, and it staring back at me; two naked pictures of some skinny white girl. I flipped them over to see what was on the back, and they were both written out to him.

At that moment I just sat there on the edge of the bed, in total shock, still gripping the pictures in my hand. I heard the shower cut off and my fiancé opening the bathroom door. I could see the door opening and a cloudy mist of steam pouring out into the bedroom…Now I will tell you here is where it gets a little fuzzy; because at this point anger has taken over my memories.

As he came around the bed, I remember asking him "What the hell is this?" His answer to me was "oh that's nothing, she is just a friend." From that point on, I remember doing a lot of crying, yelling and cussing; ending with him telling me to calm down and "it's not what I think." It's not what I think, how could it not be what I think? She is buck ass naked, straddling a chair! After that, I asked, him to take me home. The whole car ride home he was explaining himself and doing a whole lot of begging and pleading. But I never said a word; I just sat in the car crying silently. When we pulled up in front of my house, I got out of the car and didn't even look back.

How could he do this to me? What a fool I must be! Thinking that someone could truly love me and protect me! I would have been all alone and being cheated on, as I sat on some military base, in another state or even worse another country! "Where is my knight in shining amour?" "Where is my victory?" I will never have those things! I will never trust anyone again, the marriage is off PERMANENTLY!

A Prom Date

April 1992 ^(Age18)

It's been a little over a month since I last wrote in here. My relationship with my ex-fiancé is the same, we are definitely not getting married. Although we vowed to remain friends, I think the situation is too painful to remain anything. I can never find it in my heart to trust him or believe in anyone again. I am moving on for now and taking it slow and the next guy I date will definitely not be in the military.

Through all of the crazy madness, I did manage to secure a prom date. He is a senior at my high school and we have been friends since my junior year. Prom is in a few weeks and seeing that we both did not have dates, we decided to solve each other's problem by going together. I haven't a clue of what I am going to wear. I really can't afford anything fancy. My foster mother already informed me that she isn't paying for anything (no surprise there). So for now I have no help, no money, no family, but at least I have a prom date!

Mending A Broken Family

April 1992 ^(Age18)

I finally broke down and reached out to some of my biological family members today. It was a very hard pill to swallow. When I left my grandpa's house, I vowed to never to speak to them again

However, over time I came to realize that maybe back then, things had moved too fast with them; and maybe I just was not ready. I also realize that in two more months, I will virtually be on the streets, with no money and no place to go. So, when a person is faced with that predicament, they have to turn to family or trusted friends. I made the first call to my great aunt, who was pleasantly surprised to hear from me. Seeing that the conversation went well, I then called my dad, who was equally glad to hear from me. It was refreshing to talk to both of them; it also felt like a huge burden had been lifted off of me. Not to mention I missed my little sister terribly. My dad will be coming to get me in a few weeks. We will be heading to my great aunt's house for a family dinner, and I can not wait.

The Miracle on Prom Street
April 1992 (Age18)

Well, despite my foster mother's negativity, and against all odds, I am definitely going to prom! I have all the support I need. My date's parents are paying for all the tickets, my real good friend (that I hang out with at the local college radio station) is paying for my hair and nails and providing me with some spending money. My best friend is supplying the make-up lady, and finally my dad and his wife (they're not divorced and have both decided to work it out), are getting the materials so she can make my dress. I feel like Cinderella whose wish just got granted, and now she can go to the ball

Here Comes Cinderella
May 1992 (Age18)

I just got back from all of the prom festivities, boy has it been a long weekend, but I had so much fun. All of my friends looked amazing. I felt just like Cinderella! My date (who by the way is now my boyfriend), escorted me to the prom, dressed in a top hat, white gloves, jacket tails and carrying a cane. He looked so clean! My friend from the college radio station came to my house and filmed the whole thing. My hair, make-up and nails looked like I belonged in Vogue magazine! I mean seriously, I felt just like a beauty queen. Not to mention my dress was gorgeous, all black (my favorite color) with a wedding train. This is one weekend of happiness that no one will be able to take away from me! I will never forget this weekend.

My Prom Picture from May 1992 (don't laugh) ☺

My Reality Check

May 1992 (Age18)

Well, now that all of the prom madness has calmed down, I am back to facing my real reality. That reality is, there is no Cinderella and a fairy godmother is not going to show up and rescue me. I graduate in a few more weeks and turn 19. I will be officially kicked out of foster care and left out on the streets.

Quiet as kept, for the past month, I have been living with different people every week. It's not that I can't stay home, but would you want to stay somewhere, where you are not wanted or even treated like a human being? You would think that the foster care agency would have had a better plan for me. Sure my worker is great, and I did finish those ridiculous independent living classes; but those classes can't pay my rent or feed me. I work as a waitress, how can that job help to take care of me?

I thought about applying for school, but honestly, how can I afford it? I don't even know if college is right for me. I reached out to my dad, he said I could stay with him for a small rent fee; but right now his house is full to capacity, I don't even know where I would sleep. My best friend said that I can come and stay with her and her family, but I don't want to be that big of a burden on anybody. So for now only God knows where I will end up.

Most of my friends are happy gearing up for college or taking a year off to figure out where they want to be. Too bad that option can't be given to me.

I have been through so much in my life, over the years, but managed to remain strong. At this point, I would even call myself a fighter; but leaving foster care without a clue of where I am going or what I am going to do, might actually beat me. Right now, my reality is pretty unfair. I feel as if the foster care system is just dumping me. So for now I might end up a kid wandering the streets…

Graduation Day
June 1992 (Age19)

Today is my Graduation Day and true to the end my foster mother will not be there to see me. Truth be told, I had already decided a long time ago that I was not going to my graduation. That long-awaited diploma seemed pointless and a joke, if I was going to be living on the streets. Besides I have no year book, no class pictures, I have absolutely none of the graduating essentials that a senior in high school needs. Honestly, if it were not for my college radio station buddy, graduating from his college a month before me, I wouldn't even be going. He gave me his cap and gown and purchased my hat tassel for me (true friend). So today I walk, and I walk for myself and everyone who has supported me.

This is an actual picture of me, as I received my high school diploma.

My Temporary Plan

July 1992 (Age19)

As for leaving foster care this week, I have developed a temporary plan. I will be staying with my boy friend's family, in their spare room. Staying there will come with a few rules, but nothing I can't handle. The rules are simple: it has to be temporary, I have to work or either go to school, clean up after myself, and most importantly don't get pregnant. I can certainly abide by those rules, and I am definitely not trying to get pregnant! Funny thing about that is if I did get pregnant, I would get all the help that I need; housing, furniture, food, medical and even some money. It's a damn shame when you stop to think about it.

Here, I have been in foster care basically my entire life. I technically have no solid or strong bond to my biological family. I've been chained to a government-run institution (foster care), where they basically did everything for me and now they're abandoning me. They're abandoning me with no stability, no food, no housing, nothing, BUT if I get pregnant, the same agency will help me get all of those things! Now that's insanity and one of the most "ass backward" things that I have ever heard of. Anyway no babies for me, that would seriously screw up everything.

So for now, I have picked up a second job to help cover some of my expenses, and I will make sure that I follow all of the house rules to the letter. As for college, life is already too complicated, so for now college will just have to wait on me.

Searching For God Through All This Misery
July 1992 (Age19)

I even started reading my bible and praying a lot. I used to pray every day and go to church on Sundays, but I had completely stopped all of that. I figured that God had abandoned me. I think a combination of my foster mother forcing me to go to church, and me believing that every time I prayed for something, I would receive nothing, kept me from believing that God was down for me. So, I figured if I stop praying, then there will be no more room for disappointment, heartache, failure or agony. But now I am trying to find God and change the way I think. I realize that God has been there all along, I just need to slowly gravitate back to my church roots. I am now learning that a person (for whatever reason) may have to go through something horrible but God can and will eventually grant you peace.

The Problem is, I just don't know when my peace is coming, but I know that it is not coming anytime soon. I just found out that I am pregnant.

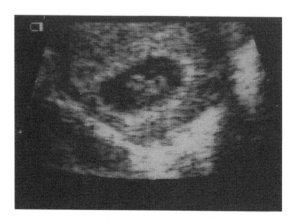

I don't know where I will end up, or how I will be. I just know that whatever happens, leaving foster care, or "aging out," is what they're calling it; what ever they call it, it won't break me.

To Be Continued... *"Aging Out of My Mind"*
Coming Soon!

Thanks for allowing me to share parts of my life with you!

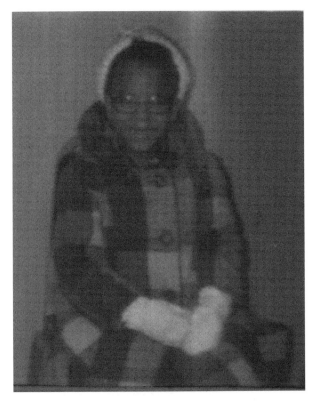

Me about age 4

For more information about the book series, or LaTasha
Please visit: www.latashacwatts.com
Facebook: LaTasha C. Watts
Twitter: LCWatts